1 The Life of a Lady

Florence Nightingale lived
in Victorian England.
Her family were rich.
Florence could have had an easy life.
But she chose to work.
She chose a very difficult job.
Why?

Florence was born in 1820.
Her parents lived in Italy.
She was named after the city
where she was born – Florence.
The family moved back to England
when Florence was one year old.

Florence had a sister.
Her name was Parthe.
Parthe was older than Florence.

The sisters grew up in a rich family.
They had two houses.
One house was in Derbyshire,
the other was in the South of England.

The girls had lots of friends.
They were happy as children.
Florence and Parthe went to lots of parties.
They also travelled abroad.
Parthe liked this life very much.

Florence was clever and good looking.
Lots of people liked her.
But Florence wanted more.
She was not content.

In Victorian times,
rich ladies did not work.
But Florence wanted to do
something useful.
She wanted to do something important.

She was also sure that God wanted
her to do something important.
When she was almost 17
she wrote in her diary:
'God spoke and called me to his service.'

She was sure she had to do
something important.
But she did not know what it was.
The call from God made her more restless.

Florence Nightingale

Sandra Woodcock

Published in association with The Basic Skills Agency

Hodder & Stoughton

A MEMBER OF THE HODDER HEADLINE GROUP

Acknowledgements

Photos: pp. 3, 9 and 19 © Popperfoto, pp. 6 and 23 © Hulton-Deutsch, pp. 13 and 27 © Camera Press, p. 17 © Corbis.
Cover: © Hulton-Deutsch.

Orders: please contact Bookpoint Ltd, 39 Milton Park, Abingdon, Oxon OX14 4TD. Telephone: (44) 01235 400414, Fax: (44) 01235 400454. Lines are open from 9.00–6.00, Monday to Saturday, with a 24 hour message answering service. Email address: orders@bookpoint.co.uk

British Library Cataloguing in Publication Data
A catalogue record for this title is available from The British Library

ISBN 0 340 71159 0

First published 1998
Impression number 10 9 8 7 6 5 4 3 2
Year 2003 2002 2001 2000 1999

Typeset by Fakenham Photosetting Ltd, Fakenham, Norfolk,
Printed in Great Britain for Hodder & Stoughton Educational, a division of Hodder Headline Plc, 338 Euston Road, London NW1 3BH, by Redwood Books, Trowbridge, Wiltshire.

Contents

2 The Dream

When Florence was 22,
she met a man called Richard Monckton-Miles.
He fell in love with her,
and wanted to marry her.
He was rich.
He was good-looking.
He was witty and kind.

Florence was in love with him.
It was a perfect match.
But Florence did not want to marry.
She wanted to be a nurse.

Her family was shocked.
Nursing was not a job for a lady.
It was one of the lowest jobs.
At that time, the only nurses were
street women, drunks and prostitutes.

Hospitals were dirty and crowded.
Beds were filthy.
There was dried blood on floors and walls.
The patients had lice.
Hospitals were not cleaned,
because nothing was known about germs.
A hospital was the last place
a lady would visit.

But Florence had always helped sick people.
She loved to visit poor people.
She read all she could about hospitals.
She made lots of notes.

She found out about good hospitals.
They were in Germany and France
and they were run by nuns.
Nursing could be a good job.
Florence was sure of that.

She got up early each morning,
to write down her ideas.
Her mother and sister were very angry.
They wanted her to give up this mad idea.

Florence Nightingale helping the soldiers.

Florence thought about nursing all the time.
She thought about it so much,
it made her ill.
She was very unhappy.

Her friends took her on holiday.
In Greece, she found a baby owl
and kept it as a pet.
She named it Athena
and brought it back to England.
She carried it around in her pocket.

But Florence could not give up
her dream of nursing.
On her holiday, she also went to Germany.
She went to a hospital there.
The hospital was run by nuns.
It was a hospital which trained nurses.

Florence stayed there for three months.
The life was hard.
She worked all day.
She worked from 5am to 7pm.
The food was poor.
But Florence was happy there.

She learned a lot about nursing.
She watched operations.
She was able to help out.
She had her own ideas about
making nursing better.

Her mother and sister thought
she was bringing shame to the family.
Florence felt as if
she was committing a crime.
But she would not give in.

At last Florence came back to England.
But she did not want to go home.
Instead, she went to work in London.
She set up a home to care for sick ladies.
She was able to practise nursing.

She even worked in the slums of Soho.
She looked after prostitutes and drunks.
Sometimes they died in her arms.

Florence had plans to do much more.
In October 1854, Florence had a letter.
The letter was to change her life.

Florence Nightingale at work during the Crimean War.

3 The Challenge

The letter was from Florence's friend.
He worked for the British Government.
The Government wanted
to help British soldiers.

The soldiers were fighting a war
against Russian soldiers.
It was called the Crimean War.
It was in Turkey.

The newspaper told stories about the war.
They told how terrible it was.
The soldiers were dying of disease.
There was cholera in the camps.
The hospital could not cope.

It was filthy.
It was too full.
The doctors did not have
what they needed.

The sick men had to come to the hospital
by ship.
The dead bodies were tipped into the sea.
They floated and rotted in the water.

It was terrible.
The letter asked Florence for help.
It asked her to take a team of nurses
to Turkey.

Florence did the best she could.
She took 38 women.
Some of them were nuns.
Many of them were rough and poor.
There were no proper nurses.

They had a long journey across Europe.
The last stage of the journey was by sea.
The ship was crawling with cockroaches.
There was a bad storm,
and Florence was sea-sick.
By the end of the sea journey
she was so ill she could not stand up.

The first things she saw on the beach were
a dead horse, and a pack of starving dogs.
The horse had been washed up on the shore.
This was not a good start.

The nurses had rooms in the hospital,
but there was hardly any furniture.
The walls were damp,
and there were rats everywhere.

The hospital was in Scutari.
There was mud all around it.
The hospital had no tables.
There was nothing to cook with.

The doctors did not want the nurses there.
The nurses wanted to help the patients.
Florence told them not to help the patients.
They must wait for a doctor to
ask them for help.

There were lots of sick
and wounded soldiers.
But Florence set the nurses other work.
They sorted bedding and made pillows.
She went to buy good food and cooking pans.

Florence Nightingale comforts a wounded soldier.

All the time more soldiers
came into the hospital in pain.
Their wounds were infected
and had maggots in them.
A lot of the men had sickness.
There were no toilets.
The men had to use pots.
There were only 20 pots for 1,000 men.

The pots were tipped into
large open tubs on the wards.
The smell was terrible.
Florence stood by the tubs
until they were taken away and emptied.
Still the doctors did not
ask for their help.

After four days there were so many patients.
The doctors had to ask for help.
Florence could show them
how useful nurses could be.

The women worked long hours
in very difficult conditions.
Florence had very little rest or sleep.
She was always busy.

Florence worked hard to make things better.
She found stores full of things.
These things should have been
in the hospital.

Soon there were more towels, shirts,
brushes, combs, kettles, pans and spoons.
The bedding was washed and boiled
to kill the lice.
The sewers were cleaned out.
She had the water supply
to the hospital checked.
They found out it was passing
over a dead horse!

Florence wrote long letters and reports
to important people.
She worked until two or three o'clock
in the morning.
She was very angry.

Men were dying in battles.
But more men were dying when they were sick.
The sick men were not being cared for.

Many of the men in charge
said she was meddling.
They did not like her.

But the soldiers on the wards
loved Florence Nightingale.
She treated them with respect,
when others said they were scum.
She stood up for them
and tried to make things better.

The 'Lady with the Lamp'.

4 Fame

In England the newspapers wrote
stories about her work.
They said she was an angel.
They called her
'The Lady with the Lamp'.
This was because
she walked the wards at night,
looking after the soldiers.
They said she was kind and gentle.

Florence was all of these things.
But she was also very tough and strong.
Few people in England could know
what she had to put up with.

Queen Victoria was told about her work.
She sent gifts to the soldiers.
She sent letters of support to Florence.
Florence was making a difference.
The death rate in hospitals was going down.

Florence Nightingale as a young woman.

At last the war ended.
Florence could go home.
She came back to England in July 1856.
There was a big party planned for her.
She was a national heroine.

But Florence hated fuss.
She came back to England in secret.
No one saw her arrive.
She took a train to Derbyshire,
and walked to her home from the station.

When she was home,
people wanted to see her.
She had many letters and invitations.
But Florence said no to all of them.
There was one invitation she did accept.
It was from Queen Victoria.

Florence did go to see the Queen.
She did not go for her own glory.
She went because she saw a chance
to help soldiers.
She talked to the Queen about change.
She talked about making the army hospitals
better in the future.
Her work would be wasted
if things went on in the same way.

She wrote to people who could do something.
She saw important men
who could change things.
She never gave up.

She wrote a long report on what she had seen
in the Crimean War.
The report said that for every man
who died in battle,
seven had died of disease.

Florence was 40 years old.
She lived to be 90.
But she was not well.
She spent most of her time lying down.
She did not let this stop her.

She wrote letters and reports
and met anyone who could help her.
Slowly, change came.
The army medical schools became better.
Florence also said that the soldiers
should have education and sport,
so they did not turn to drink.

5 Nightingale Nurses

When Florence went to the Crimea,
The Times newspaper set up a fund.
People gave lots of money to
the Florence Nightingale Fund.
She wanted to use the money
to start a Training School for nurses.

She had written books
on hospitals and nursing.
Her plans for hospital buildings were good.
There should be plenty of space
and fresh air.
Most of all, hospitals should be clean.

She began the first training for nurses.
Many doctors thought it was a waste of time.
To them, a nurse was like a maid.
She did only basic jobs
and did not need teaching.
But Florence Nightingale set out to show
that nurses could be important helpers.

Florence Nightingale at Scutari.

The school for nurses was set up in
St. Thomas's hospital in London.
There were 15 student nurses.
They had to train for a year.
They had to be very well-behaved.
A nurse who flirted with a doctor
was dismissed right away.
They had to pass exams.

Soon doctors saw that nurses
could be skilled helpers.
This was the start of modern nursing.
It was the end of the old idea
that nursing was not a good job.
Florence Nightingale's ideas were used
all over the world for training nurses.

6 The Work Goes On

Florence was 40
when the training school started.
She lived for another 50 years.
All that time she kept working.

She still wanted to make things better
for British soldiers.
She cared about them all over the world.

There were soldiers in India.
They were living in bad conditions.
Florence found out a lot about India.
She became an expert on the army there.
She spoke to a lot of important people.
She asked them to make things better
for the soldiers.

In 1907, Florence was 87 years old.
The King gave her a medal.
It was called the Order of Merit.
It was for all her good work.

She died three years later.
She was 90 years old.
But her name and work live on.

Florence worked hard all her life.